COMPLETE GUIDE ON COVER LETTER

COVER LETTER

Best to solve all cover letter issues

Why You Should Read This Book

THIS BOOK IS ABOUT ALL ASPECT OF COVER LETTER.

DO'S AND DON'TS, WORDS TO INCLUDES

Table of Contents

What is a Cover Letter

Cover letter refers to a brief explanation letter before the official document. For example, if you want to send a document through the fax, an attached cover letter is needed, in order to explain the reason why you must send it by using some brief words. It is not merely using in the application letter, but also has a board application scope. However, it is related to the employment.

When you are seeking for a job, a cover letter is an instrument which can indicate the employment advertise/employer/ address, and it also includes the information about where you found the advertisement; what you bring to the company; why you suit this job; and also your understanding of the company. Cover letters play an important role when paired with a resume. It's a letter you need to pay much attention to. It is really important for your job hunting.

A cover letter is the 'cherry on top' of a job application and shows that you have taken the time and consideration to walk your potential employer through your best assets as a preview to the actual CV.

A covering letter should be used to introduce yourself and explain why you are applying to the post, which post you are applying to, and why you are better suited than the thousand other applicants to the post! You should always find the name of the person who will be reading your application. It is much more personal to do this than to use a generic ' To the manager' or 'To whom it may concern' and shows you have gone to some effort. It is the small touches like this which will impress upon the employer how much more effort you have gone to than the competition in researching and applying for the post to which you are interested.

Obviously you should have the required skills and knowledge to do the job or if not then the enthusiasm to learn quickly and be of use in your new post. If you are applying to a post to which you are under qualified you need to explain this in your covering letter. Perhaps you are having a career change and have found some enthusiasm for a new direction. This may or may not be acceptable to the employer and they might simply ignore an application from someone who is unqualified for the job. However if you draw on your other experiences and paint yourself in a brilliant light, explaining what your other talents and skills will bring to the role, you may well win them over.

You should always paint yourself in the best possible light, whatever your experiences, when writing a covering letter. Include reasons for applying to the job, your most relevant skills, qualifications, experiences and previous employments. A cover letter should really not be more than a single side of paper and will tell the interviewer everything they need to know in a brief, concise manner. When closing do so in a grateful manner and always request an interview. Use good quality paper and type out your application if possible.

In short a cover letter allows the employer to quickly sift through many applications and decide which are heading for the top and which are heading for the waste paper bin.

Application letter is a cover letter because it serves as the cover of the résumé. It is also considered a business letter because of its nature. This letter is used to negotiate further for the applicant to enter a company as an additional manpower. It could also be considered as a sales letter because the applicant is trying to sell himself to the company by way of compensation if given the chance to get hired.

Cover letter varies on its purposes and all of them are all covering a more vivid presentation of the matter to be discussed or offered.

Why are cover letters important?

When too little time is spent creating a cover letter, it basically gets a once over by the recruiter and put into a discard file or a trash email folder. This is unfortunate, because the cover letter and resume are the one and only chance that you have to create a bond with the employer.

The letter is the personalized portion of an otherwise impersonal document, your resume. A well written letter prepares the reader to accept your resume as something to warrant considerable attention. It is only when your two documents work well together and convey the appropriate message, that interviews, and eventually job offers, will arise.

When a potential employer opens the envelope, your cover letter should be the first thing that is seen. The letter should make a memorable first impression; it sets the mood for your application, and can guarantee that your resume gets the thoughtful inspection that it deserves. The higher that you climb up the professional ladder, the more important cover letters, and other types of letters written during a job search, will be. This is especially true for candidates who must show written communication abilities as part of their daily responsibilities (really that applies to nearly everyone). Cover letters are a very important instrument for exhibiting crucial job skills. If you don't convey the appropriate message here, the door to your opportunities with this employer could likely be slammed shut. However, if you do a good job, it will help you to stand out from your competition.

A small minority of people like some veteran recruiters mistakenly believe that you can do without great cover letters. They could not be more wrong. Many of these folks simply dislike receiving poorly written generic cover letters. The absence of a letter of introduction clearly signifies a lack of desire on your part to any employer. If writing and marketing yourself effectively is not strength, simply use a pro resume writer to help. The best cover letters will distinguish you as a serious candidate worthy of an interview.

Your resume should be strictly business and 100% factual. Cover letters however, are the place to emphasize all of your less tangible attributes, which may not necessarily fit into the skills, talents and abilities area of your resume. Isn't having a consistent positive attitude over a long term stay at an employer very important? Isn't having the vision, faith and ability to think big critical in many professions? Isn't confidence an asset?

Frankly, there are many intangibles that contribute significantly to why one candidate would easily be the better choice among many similar candidates with otherwise equal qualifications. Your cover letter is the place to separate yourself from others and sell all of your assets to an employer. The concept of a cover letter is as old as the hills. For example, in 1482, Leonardo DaVinci wrote a bold cover (sales) letter to the Duke of Milan to create his own employment opportunity and it worked. Certainly, over the years society and technology has advanced, but this timeless strategy remains widely successful, if your cover letters are well written they will help you get hired.

A great cover letter also can ideally reveal the single most important consideration for an employer, that would be who referred you. You can bet if it is one of his friends, family or employees it will definitely strengthen your case. Employers always believe in minimizing any risks especially when it comes to hiring, hence the interviews, background checks, credit checks, drug tests and aptitude testing routine. Therefore, it stands to reason; the ultimate door opener would be a personal referral from his inner circle. Why all this careful screening of candidates for employment?

Because the only real motivation for hiring a new employee is it allows the employer to earn three to five times the employee's salary in profits. Basically, it is all business and return on investment. Therefore, when a hiring goes wrong, it also costs the company significant profits as well. Thus, let your resume brag about all of your experience, but keep your cover letter reserved for why you are and will continue to be a great contributor to the employer you have targeted. While it may be very challenging to think about things from your potential employer's point of view, this is one of the most effective secrets to writing a great cover letter with a powerful call to action.

Powerful cover letters open doors to previously unattainable employers who seldom if ever need to advertise job opportunities. They deem you as safe to hire because you have the inside track with a referral from the employer's trusted inner circle. They separate (free) you from the other thousands of equally well qualified candidates in the employer's mind. They demonstrate your passion and true desire for the job and have a strong call to action so you will get more interviews. Finally, they build your value in the mind of the very Hiring Manager with whom you will soon be interviewing. A job search without them can be mission impossible.

Just how important is a resume cover letter? To answer that question, imagine yourself to be the employer. You've just had a busy day packed with tons and tons of work, and now, as the day is drawing to a close, you're about to sift through a stack of applications for a job vacancy in your office. You need to act fast, because your office cannot afford to operate and go on another day without this position being filled.

The pile looks mighty high and with droopy shoulders, you start going through all the papers before you. Now, are you really going to have to read all of them page by page? No way, unless you're willing to spend the rest of the night just doing it. The fact is, you will most likely read only the front page and quickly filter all nicely-written, attention-grabbing application from the dull-looking ones that don't seem to fit the bill. That quick. And maybe when you're down to the final ten applications, that's when you start actually considering the 'meat' of these bulky applications.

So, just how important is a resume cover letter? As important as your actual qualifications for the job. What most job seekers fail to realize is that employers do not actually take much time on reading through all those resumes page by page. This is especially true now since the economy is heading for the gutter. For a single job position available, there are hundreds, even thousands, of qualified individuals vying for it. You would be hard-pressed to get noticed by the employers, let alone win their total attention.

If you want to have a fighting chance in securing that job, you need to work really hard on your cover letter. The cover letter is the first thing that employers look into when evaluating an applicant. It is where you personally address the employers and talk to them about who you are and what you can do. One of the biggest mistakes you'll ever commit when applying for a job is sending an application with just your resume and nothing else. This is impersonal at best, and it shows how unprofessional and haphazard you are.

When written brilliantly, the cover letter can work wonders for you. There have been many claims of people actually grabbing a job because of how well they presented themselves in their cover letter. Some who may not even be qualified for a job were able to land it because their cover letters made up for what they lack. Resume cover letters, when written properly and with an enthusiastic spirit, can actually "stretch" the truth about you.

Cover letters are something you can't do without. What you write on it, or if you've even prepared one in the first place, speaks volumes about you. It tells the employer about who you are at a very quick glance. It tells them that you are a human being who is personable and very much willing to take on the job.

Cover letters are the introduction of your resume and of you. They set the stage for what the reader is going to see on your resume and also will tell a recruiter or hiring manager if they want to read your resume.

A great introductory letter conveys a high level professionalism and shows the hiring manager that you're interested in their position and why you are the best candidate for the job. This is why it is always important to present a completely customized version. Anyone can write a blanket cover letter but you should always focus yours on the position and company that you want to interview you. It shows time, dedication, and interest.

Having a cover letter that clearly defines why you want the position and why you are the best candidate for the position speaks volumes for you as a candidate. it should include the company's name, the hiring manager's name and contact information if you have it, the position you are applying to, and a description of why you are the best candidate for the position. I would not advise writing in the cover letter 'I am the best candidate for the position because...' but rather specifically state accomplishments or contributions that you have made in your previous jobs that align with the main points the employer is looking for in this position.

As the employer scans through it they should say I like what I'm reading and this person sounds like they might be a good fit, let me read through their resume to get some additional information.

Every job seeker needs a strong cover letter and one that can be customized to different positions as you apply. Consider having a professional design one for you that can be easily altered to each position and company you want to apply to and is strong enough to catch the reader's attention and make them want to read your resume.

Let me put it this way: What would happen if you had THE perfect résumé, but then sent along an accompanying cover letter that had grammatical, spelling and punctuation errors? What if you didn't express thoughts in a clear, compelling way? How would an employer respond to this? If you guessed not favorably, you are right!

Proofreading errors in a cover letter are the number one job prospect killer for résumés and applications. In fact, the same rules for résumés apply for cover letters. They HAVE to be perfect. Cover letters are in equal standing to résumés for the very reason that it tells a lot about a candidate that a résumé can't communicate.

Whereas a résumé is usually presented more in the abbreviated or 'telegraph' style of communication, a cover letter is a premier demonstration of your professional writing skills... much along the lines of how an employer might expect you to communicate via email messages or letters on their behalf, should you come under their employment.

Another key clue to prospective employers that a cover letter delivers is an understanding about the candidate that goes beyond the words on the page. Does the applicant actually 'get' what the employer is seeking in applicants for this particular position?

I recall one applicant who sent in a fairly qualified résumé paired with a cover letter that addressed the position we were recruiting, but the person clearly 'elevated' themselves to a much higher management role than what the position mandated. It was very clear that there was a disconnect between what the person's perception of the job duties were, and the ones being sought after.

6 Examples of Cover Letters for different jobs

RECEPTIONIST COVER LETTER SAMPLE

Cover letter sample

July 27, 2017
Mr. Wendell Simpson
HR Manager
ABC Corporation
55 Custer Pkwy.
Sometown, PA 55555
Re: Front-Office Receptionist, Advertised on Monster

Dear Mr. Simpson:

After reviewing your job announcement for a front-office receptionist, I was struck by how closely my qualifications match your requirements.

For the past 3 years, I have worked as a front-office receptionist at XYZ, Inc. (a medical device company), where my duties are very similar to those outlined in your position opening:

- Warmly greeting and assisting customers and visitors

- Providing prompt, courteous call handling, routing and screening within a busy office setting

- Assisting HR with maintaining updated company rosters and phone lists

- Using MS Office to develop reports, templates, spreadsheets and presentations

I believe that past performance is one of the best predictors of future success. Here are excerpts from my most recent review at XYZ:

"…Christina is a tremendous asset to our team in her role as front-office receptionist…energetic, enthusiastic and upbeat… outstanding communication and customer service skills… highly organized and efficient…her computer skills have been a real asset to the department…reliable, flexible and willing to pitch in when needed…a team player and outstanding employee. We are all going to miss her!"

— Penelope Cho, Supervisor, XYZ, Inc.

Next month I will be relocating to Sometown, PA, making it impractical for me to remain at XYZ due to the 100-mile commute. I have given my employer 30-day notice of my resignation, and am actively seeking employment in what will soon be my new hometown.

I am available to interview in person with just a few days notice, or immediately over the phone or via Skype (Skype ID: christinanicholslive). I hope to hear from you soon.

Sincerely,
Christina Nichols

Enclosure: Résumé

COSTUMER SERVICE COVER LETTER SAMPLE

Vera Jones
Sometown, CT 55555 | (555) 555-5555 | vj@somedomain.com
July 27, 2017
Ms. Wendy Solomon
Human Resources Specialist
XYZ Company
55 Seabreeze Ave.
Sometown, CT 55555

Dear Ms. Solomon:

Your customer service manager position advertised on Monster is an excellent fit to my qualifications.

During the past five years, I have been promoted to increasingly responsible positions within ABC Company, serving as a customer service representative, acting supervisor and East Coast customer service manager (my current role). Throughout my tenure with ABC, I have built lasting customer relationships, salvaged key accounts and strengthened customer loyalty.

Regarded as a proactive problem solver and liaison between cross-functional business units and high-value client accounts,

I am passionate about serving customers with excellence. Achievement highlights:

- Rebuilt the East Coast customer service team from the ground-up. Instituted new training programs, accountability measurements and performance goals that led to record-setting gains in customer satisfaction scores¾from 85% in 2016 to 96% in 2017.

- Averted the threatened loss of three multimillion-dollar accounts. Investigated and resolved billing discrepancies and rectified shipping delays to win back client trust. Worked with cross-functional teams to improve accounting and logistics processes to prevent future issues.

- Rolled out a new CRM system to allow for more personalized and customized service.

My customer service management experience is reinforced by a bachelor's degree in communications, proficiencies in CRM database systems and fluency in Spanish.

I am confident in my ability to further the success of your customer service organization. Please call me at (555) 555-5555 or email vj@somedomain.com to arrange a meeting. I look forward to speaking with you.

Sincerely,
Vera Jones

Enclosure: Résumé

EXECUTIVE ASSISTANCE COVER LETTER SAMPLE

Brett Chandler
Sometown, CO 55555 | (555) 555-5555 | bc@somedomain.com
July 27, 2017
Ms. Sarah Smith
HR Manager
ABC Corporation
800 12th Ave.
Sometown, CO 55555
Re: Executive Assistant | Job Ref. #55555 | Advertised on Monster

Dear Ms. Smith:

Many people view executive assistants as glorified secretaries, and while there's nothing wrong with secretarial work, my view of this position is different. Yes, I perform secretarial tasks (quite well!), but I see my role as a key business partner¾vital to the success of the executive team, department and company.

I am your secret weapon, working diligently to ensure goals are met and daily operations run smoothly.

For the past five years, I have served as executive assistant to the regional VP of a major insurance company. Previously during my employment with a regional credit union, I rapidly advanced through roles as an office assistant and secretary to become executive assistant to the SVP of HR.

These experiences allow me to wear the many "hats" required to be a value-adding executive assistant. I've earned repeated accolades for my strengths in…

- Managing multiple high-priority projects with competing deadlines

- Creating reports, spreadsheets, budgets and PowerPoint presentations

- Coordinating executive travel, schedules and calendars

- Handling sensitive and confidential matters with discretion

- Planning and overseeing logistics for meetings, tradeshows and events

- Assisting with payroll, new-hire orientation, benefits enrollment and other HR functions

My qualifications are reinforced by credentials that include an AA in business; an in-progress BA in HR administration; and an advanced command of MS Office, SAP and Oracle.

You may reach me at (555) 555-5555 or email bc@somedomain .com to set up a meeting. Thank you for your time.

Sincerely,
Brett Chandler
Enclosure: Résumé

IT COVER LETTER SAMPLE

Maria Frankel
Sometown, DE 55555 | (555) 555-5555 | mf@somedomain.com
July 27, 2017
Mr. Thomas Jones
HR Manager
ABC Corp
15 Elm Street
Sometown, DE 55555
Re: IT Helpdesk Technician, Advertised on Monster

Dear Mr. Jones:

I am interested in joining your tier 1 helpdesk team. A longtime fan of ABC Corp's commitment to customer service, I bring to the table a strong customer service mindset combined with technical skills honed throughout my 15 years of helpdesk experience.

Key strengths include:

- High-volume ticket management. In my current position as helpdesk support specialist for XYZ Co, I handle 1,725+ tickets per month, fully resolving and documenting issues for future reference.

- A track record of consistently meeting or exceeding performance targets correlated with call handling and customer satisfaction goals.

- Technical knowledge:

- Windows (all versions); Windows Server 2003, 2008 R2 and 2012; macOS; Unix

- Microsoft Active Directory Services

- LAN, WAN and WiFi network technology (DNS, DHCP, NTP, SNMP and Nagios)

- MS Office 365/Exchange

- Recognition for exceptional service delivery through "ACE Team Member" awards.

Mr. Jones, if you are seeking an experienced, tech-savvy and customer service-oriented helpdesk technician with the proven ability to establish excellent relationships with customers, employees, vendors and manufacturers, we should speak.

I look forward to learning more about this position and can be reached at (555) 555-5555 or mf@somedomain.com. Thank you for your time.

Sincerely,
Maria Frankel

Enclosure: Résumé

MANAGER COVER LETTER SAMPLE

Patrick Abrams

1704 Maple Ave. | Sometown, IN 47250 | (555) 555-5555 | pat@anydomain.com

Ms. Katy Smith

Director of Distribution Operations

Acme Inc.

2000 Industrial Ave.

Sometown, IN 47250

Re: Warehouse Manager (Job #: 5587), advertised on Monster

Dear Ms. Smith:

I was intrigued when I found your warehouse manager job posting, as I know I could positively contribute to your operation. Since earning my promotion to warehouse manager for XYZ Company's 35,000-square-foot distribution center three years ago, I have received consistent commendations for achieving gains in productivity, safety and efficiency — accomplished during a time of significant budget cuts.

Your warehouse operation would benefit from my proven success in:

- Launching 5S and other lean-manufacturing programs to elevate the efficiency and effectiveness of the distribution center.

- Overseeing inventory management, stock controls, pick/ pack operations, and order processing for high-volume shipping and receiving operations.

- Supervising and scheduling unionized workforces of up to 20 employees per shift within a 24x7 environment.

- Upgrading SAP warehouse management systems to improve inventory management and distribution accuracy.

- Developing and leading training programs to improve employee productivity, job satisfaction and workplace morale.

- Accelerating order fulfillment to achieve a 28% reduction in order-processing time, which helped retain and grow business from key accounts.

I recently learned that my employer plans to close the Indianapolis distribution center later this year. It offered me a warehouse manager position at its Minneapolis site, but family responsibilities prevent me from relocating at this time.

If you agree that my qualifications perfectly match your requirements, please call me at (555) 555-5555 to arrange an interview. Thank you for considering my credentials, and I look forward to learning more about this exciting opportunity.

Sincerely,
Patrick Abrams

Enclosure: Resume

TEACHER COVER LETTER SAMPLE

Winifred Thompson
55 Oak St., Sometown, OH 44101 | 216-555-5555 | winifred@
somedomain.com
Dr. Loretta Smith
Superintendent
ABC Public Schools
55 School Lane
Sometown, OH 44101

Dear Dr. Smith:

Ever since I started teaching at the elementary school level, I have been passionate in my commitment to three things: maximizing individual student performance, inspiring students' interest in technology and instilling a sense of self-worth among all students. I have dedicated my career to each of these pursuits, as my enclosed resume will attest.

That's why I was excited to see the advertisement on Monster for an elementary teacher in your district. ABC Public Schools has earned a positive reputation for celebrating diversity, achieving academic excellence and using technology as a learning tool. It would be an honor to teach your students and serve a district that maintains high educational standards and provides students with opportunities for personal growth.

My qualifications include 12 years of elementary teaching experience, MEd and BS degrees in elementary education, and a current senior professional educator (middle childhood) license in the state of Ohio.

In my most recent position as elementary educator for DEF Public School District, I developed and taught 4th and 5th grade curricula. For more than 10 years, I provided effective classroom management, creative lesson plans, detailed student evaluations and highly praised instructional delivery. As an enthusiastic volunteer, I founded and grew the school's after-school technology club, an innovative program that covered diverse technology areas -- from Internet security best practices to PowerPoint tutorials. The program became so popular that it was the school's only after-school program that was consistently filled to capacity.

Although I enjoyed my tenure at DEF Public School District, my position was eliminated last May following a round of layoffs. I am eager to resume my teaching career and would be delighted to interview for this opportunity. Please feel free to contact me at 216-555-5555 or email winifred@somedomain.com to set up a meeting.

Thank you for your interest and consideration. I look forward to hearing from you soon.

Sincerely,
Winifred Thompson

Enclosures: Resume, three reference letters, proof of licensure and college transcripts

Phrases to include when targeting your prospective employer

- The reason why you sent the resume. It was not a good choice when you send a resume without it. Write what you want specifically, and let the reader know your aim. This is really important.

- Let the reader interest in it. Try your best to introduce your education back ground, leadership, experience. Take some examples if you have.

- Show your attitude. It must be very well to indicate your personality, enthusiasm, and the confidence. Tyr to persuade them you are the best one and they should not miss you.

At last, do not forget to sign personally including your name. State your enclosures such as your attached resume, academic results or references.

To was a place I wanted work.

phrase like that probably wouldn't get you very far at a bank, but this could:

The first time I scanned a check with my smartphone I was delighted by how simple deposits suddenly became. Now that I am in the market for a job, I immediately though of Chase because I want to help to create the tools that make banking a pleasure.

These statements compliment the company. They show that you know detail about the company, so you're not just applying abitrarily. They show that you appreciate the work the company does and they provide insight into who you are and what you care about. When you're writing your cover letter, knowing your audience can help you do this. You may be applying for a job because you want any job, but that doesn't mean you can't do a little research and find something you like and respect about your prospective employer. Doing so will give you the opportunity to connect with them in a very brief moment and help you avoid getting stacked in a pile of generic applicants.

The number one best way to get someone to look at your resume closely: come across as a human being, not a list of jobs and programming languages. Tell me a little story. "I've spent the last three weeks looking for a job at a real software company, but all I can find are cheezy web design shops looking for slave labor." Or, "We yanked our son out of high school and brought him to Virginia. I am not going to move again until he is out of high school, even if I have to go work at Radio Shack or become a Wal*Mart greeter." (These are slightly modified quotes from two real people.)

Who you are matters. It's true that some companies are mostly interested in hiring people who will simply get the work done, accept a low salary, and never complain, if you're applying for a job you're actually going to like then chances are you matter. Put a little of yourself into the cover letter. You're not sharing your disease history. You're sharing your personality in a way that's relevant to the job you want. It's fun. It's an excuse to be honest, and you increase your chances of getting a job, too.

Show, Don't Tell

The best way to do this is look back on your work history — or even something relevant that you created outside of your professional life — that made you feel proud of what you can do. Tell a story about that in a few short sentences:

For her 9th birthday, my daughter wanted brownies just like the ones they make at her favorite restaurant. I accidentally spilled a little pudding mix into the batter, only to discover a trick that made one of the best desserts I've ever had. I can replicate a recipe like the best of them, but it's the mistakes I've made while baking that remind me of how much I love it.

You can tell anyone anything, but you have to provide an example to demonstrate why they should believe your claims.

Demonstrate What Every Employer Wants to Know

Most employers care about the following three things above all else:

- You're smart.

- You'll get things done.

- You'll fit in well with their corporate culture.

Before you sign and send your cover letter, do your best to ensure those three things are implied. Again, you don't ever want to actually say them, but you want your reader to think them when they've finished reading your letter.

Phrases when contacting recruitment agencies

"I am very excited to learn more about this opportunity and share how I will be a great fit for XYZ Corporation." Strong cover letter closings are enthusiastic and confident. You want the reader to have the impression you are truly passionate about the position and working for their company. This statement will also illustrate your ability to fit into the company culture and how your personality and work ethic is exactly what they're looking for.

"I believe this is a position where my passion for this industry will grow because of the XYZ opportunities you provide for your employees." It's always a good idea to explain what you find attractive about working for the company and how you want to bring your passions to the table. By doing this, you can illustrate how much thought you dedicated to applying for the position and how much you care about becoming a part of the company.

"If I am offered this position, I will be ready to hit the ground running and help XYZ Company exceed its own expectations for success." By adding this piece to your conclusion, you will be able to add some flare and excitement to your cover letter.

The reader will become intrigued by your enthusiasm to "hit the ground running." Employers look for candidates who are prepared for the position and are easy to train. Therefore, this phrase will definitely raise some curiosity and the reader will want to discover what you have to offer for their company.

"I would appreciate the opportunity to meet with you to discuss how my qualifications will be beneficial to your organization's success." Remember, you want to make it clear in your cover letter how the employer will benefit from your experience and qualifications. You want to also express how your goal is to help the organization succeed, not how the position will contribute to your personal success.

"I will call you next Tuesday to follow up on my application and arrange for an interview." The most essential part of your closing is your "call to action" statement. Remember, the purpose of your cover letter is to land an interview. Don't end your cover letter saying you'll hope to get in touch. Explain to the reader the exact day and how you will be contacting them. When you state you will be following up with the employer, make sure you do it!

Buzzwords to include

Address the cover letter to the hiring professional leading the job search if possible. That is much more likely to get the reader's attention than the generic "To Whom It May Concern" opening.

Include buzzwords from the job posting. You can often do this in a paragraph explaining why you are a match for the opening. For instance, "I have 12 years of experience strengthening accounts payable, accounts receivable, payroll, and expense control practices that captured over $5 million in savings for ABC Company" for an accounting position seeking someone with extensive A/R, A/P, and payroll experience.

Highlight three or four achievements relevant to the position. Using bullets points to bring attention to those feats is an effective method to set out the details. The bullets should persuade the reader to continue learning more about you and generate interest in reading the attached resume.

Aside from including important keywords, LinkedIn's career expert Nicole Williams recommends focusing on the craft of the first, second and third sentence. The first should be about the employer, the second should be about you and the third should be about the company. She also highly recommends resisting common clichés.

"It's not 'I'm organized,' it's not 'I'm responsible,'" she tells Mashable. "People would expect you to be anyway."

Find a way to rephrase those overused words. Instead of saying "I'm a hard worker," say "I have an enormous capacity for work" (one of Williams' current employees began her cover letter with that line, and was hired instantly).

When directly talking about the employer, Williams says these key words are great: admire, inspired by and listen. When describing yourself, Williams recommends: enthusiastic, passionate and integrity.

Javid Muhammedali, the vice president of product management at Monster, tells Mashable that keywords change depending on the job you're applying for. However, for a general cover letter, he said these following words connote key skills that work for "all resumes with 0-4 years of experience."

• Administrative Skills

• Communication Skills

• Computer Skills

• Customer Relations

• Microsoft Office and Outlook

• Multitasking

- Problem Solving Skills

- Resolve Customer Issues

Keywords are crucial to get past an applicant tracking system ("Otherwise known as the black hole you submit your resume into online," says Vicki Salemi, a career expert and author of two advice books). One of the simplest things you can do is reflect the job description.

"Highlight the skills and experiences they need by referencing the job description and inserting the exact words into your letter," she tells Mashable. "If they're hiring a valuation manager with experience in calculating intangible assets, ensure you put 'intangible assets.'"

Aside from that, Salemi also recommends powerful verbs that will "pack a punch."

- Launched

- Led

- Managed

- Analyzed

- Achieved

- Budgeted

- Forecasted

- Ignited

- Navigated

- Negotiated

- Reorganized

- Rescued

- Identified

- Generated

EXAMPLE OF WORDS

Examples of skill keywords include wrote, analyzed, quantified, planned, programmed, designed, created, built, taught and trained.

Examples of results-oriented keywords include: increased, reduced, redesigned, upgraded, initiated, implemented, reformulated, generated and produced.

Examples of recognition related keywords include honored, awarded, promoted, selected, lauded for, received a bonus for, recognized, chosen and credited.

14 things to avoid saying

• **It's Too Long**

Everyone learns how to write a 500-word, one-page essay in school. To most of us, it sounds like "the bare minimum." But for a cover letter, it's way too much—and will only serve to annoy the hiring manager.

The solution: Keep it Simple, Direct, Clear, and Short

Aim for 250 words. According to the Orange County Resume Survey, almost 70% of employers either want a half page cover letter (250 words) or "the shorter the better" approach.

If that seems short, just remember: All you really need to include in your cover letter is the job you want to fill, the reason you can do the job, and how you intend to do the job — with a little flair of personality. No need to write out your whole resume. No need to pen your personal manifesto. Keep it short and sweet for the hiring manager who's reading through dozens of these.

- It's Overly Formal

Too many cover letters have sentences that read like this: "I wish to convey my interest in filling the open position at your fine establishment."

Is that so, Mr. Shakespeare?

The problem with this stilted and unnatural language is that it's off-putting to hiring managers: It makes you seem insincere and even robotic, not anything like the friendly, approachable, and awesome-to-work-with person that you are.

The solution: Use Common Language and Speech Patterns

Skip the frills, and just use clear language —"I'm thrilled to be writing to apply for the [position] at [company]." You can sense that this sentence has a much more genuine and friendly tone than the first example. Here are some other complicated terms and their simpler, more natural synonyms:

- Advantageous — helpful

- Erroneous — wrong

- Leverage or utilize — use

- Attempted — tried

- Subsequently — after or later

There are a couple ways to spot overly formal language in your cover letter. First, try reading it out loud to see if there are areas that feel unnatural coming off the tongue, and rework them to flow better. You can also try using a program like Hemmingway App to help you identify over-complicated language in your writing.

- It Sounds Disingenuous

All career advisors will tell you to target your cover letter . Unfortunately, too many people think that this simply means writing something like "I love [insert target company here]."

I've got news: That's simply not good enough to show a hiring manager your enthusiasm for a company.

The solution: Demonstrate Your Understanding of the Company With Details

Instead, you'll need to read enough about the company to make a truly personalized comment in your cover letter. First, you should study the content, advertising, branding, business strategies, and culture of the company. Pay especially close attention to the department you'd like to join. Find out what the team is doing and how they're doing it, and take note of the areas that you know you can contribute to.

Including that specific information in the cover letter shows that you're interested and already have ideas for how you can help the company. So let's say that you're applying for an internship position at a company like The Muse. You might say something like:

I really enjoy reading the productivity section on The Daily Muse— it's got a great blend of psychological and technical tips, many of which I've taken to heart. I'm a sucker for this type of "food for thought" material, so I have my own ideas and resources that would make me a strong contributor in this vertical.

- You're Underselling Yourself

If you have any lines in your cover letter that read like these, you must remove them:

I'm probably not the most qualified candidate…

I'm sure you have many other more qualified candidates who have applied…

Give me a chance to prove myself…

Why would the hiring manager not hire the most qualified candidate? That would be absurd!

The solution: Make an Argument for Yourself

Even if you feel under-qualified, put on a brave face and tell the hiring manager the attributes that would make you a strong candidate. Respond to the job description, and play up the directly related and transferable skills you have that would allow you to meet the challenge.

For instance, someone applying for an entry-level position as a salesperson might write:

During college, I was responsible for ad sales in our newspaper, The Blue and Gold. I learned how to create, manage, and maintain professional relationships with business owners around our campus. My direct efforts led to a 10% profit margin increase over the year, and I believe that those skills can be directly applied to your open position.

If you're still unsure, check out career counselor Lily Zhang's suggestions for drawing out your strengths instead of your weaknesses.

Of course, remember that having too much bombast ("I'm absolutely the best and you better believe it!") also isn't good.

- It Sounds Selfish

The following is one of the most important rules to remember about writing your cover letter: It isn't just about you.

In other words, avoid writing about how working at your target company will create a great boost for your resume and career. Hiring managers are fully aware of that. What they need to know is how you're going to provide a boost for the company.

The solution: Ask What You Can Do for the Company

Your cover letter should state what you can do for the company. Ask yourself—what is it about your education and experience that would allow you to meet the challenges of the open job position? How can you leverage your expertise for the benefit of the company? What ideas do you have to move the business forward?

It's perfectly fine to mention that being hired would be mutually beneficial—the hiring manager wouldn't want you to be a demoralized worker in a role that doesn't suit your career prospects. Just keep it to a quick sentence and then move on to wooing the reader with what you can do for the company.

- It's Full of Irrelevant Filler

Got a paragraph about your semester abroad, or some other travel experience where you found your "true calling?" You should probably delete it. Do you have sentences like, "I am a hard working, efficient, and loyal person?" Don't make a series of lists of positive sounding words about yourself. It's not convincing.

Most importantly, if you've included personal information about your religion, marital status, or race, delete it. Even if you think it's adding personality, it's actually irrelevant to the job and could cause you to be discriminated against.

The solution: Focus on Your Relevant Skills and History

Only talk about the experiences that directly relate to your skills and abilities that will help you succeed in the position. So if you learned a relevant skill while you were abroad, like a language? Then it's perfectly fine to bring it up.

You should also make sure to show the hiring manager proof of your skills rather than simply say that you have them. For any word you choose to describe yourself, make sure to include an example from your work experience to back up your claim.

For example, instead of saying that you're "hard-working" or "a problem solver," write something like:

I felt like my own training could have been better, so I took the initiative to create new documents and checklists to make employee training less resource-intensive, which led to shorter training periods and faster content production.

- **It Has Too Much Information About College Metrics**

This may be strange to hear, but here are four things that don't really factor in your cover letter: the university you attended , your GPA, the classes you took, or your senior thesis.

You should be proud of yourself if you got into an Ivy League school and have a great GPA, but in most cases, they aren't great metrics for determining whether you'll be a strong employee.

The solution: Stick to Activities and Responsibilities

To the greatest extent possible, talk about activities you participated in both inside and outside of college that have some relevance to the job. A student with a 2.9 GPA but with experience as editor of a college newspaper is still very likely to get an interview for a media job.

The reason that activities speak louder than statistics is because they act as proof that you have the soft skills necessary to be a good employee and co-worker. Activities provide experience you can use to show that you are organized, have leadership skills, can work in a team, and can easily get used to a professional environment.

Above all, activities show that you were motivated to succeed beyond simply earning a degree.

By fixing these seven mistakes, your application will stand out from the sea of other entry-level candidates jockeying for the same position. A genuine, refreshing, and smart cover letter is sometimes all it takes to get attention — and kick start your career.

- Misspelled Words or Bad Grammar

While spell-check is good, it doesn't catch everything - there could be a word that's spelled right, but not the right word for the context of the sentence. Keep that spell-check in action but don't rely on it exclusively. Misspellings can be the death of your application, no matter how qualified you might be. Think of how embarrassing it would be if you have been a mechanical engineer for 30 years and spell it 'michanical' engineer on your resume. Lots of times we accidentally misspell words that are actually words themselves i.e. "manger" instead of "manager".

There can be other consequences, as well-misspelled words could interfere with resumes being found in the key word search of a resume database. So, proofread your resume yourself - it's important.

*Be sure to keep tenses consistent and check for the correct word usage (such as "counsel" versus "council").

Using a Vague Job Focus

- Be clear on the type of position you want to target - your resume should be geared toward that. If you just say "Medical Field" or "Manufacturing," the reader does not know what type of position you want, so your resume will probably not be considered. Make sure you are specific as to the type of job you want, such as "Accounting Professional", "Senior Management Executive", or "Educator."

- Not Including your Personal Brand, or your Value

In today's challenging job market, showing your uniqueness - your personal brand; and letting potential employers see the value you bring to a new position is essential. Your resume must reflect why an employer should pick up the phone and call you for an interview over the hundreds of other resumes sitting on their desk. You ultimately get hired for the value you contribute to a company, so make sure it shows on your resume.

- Making Reference to Political or Religious Organizations

A GIANT NO-NO!! Don't scare off prospective employers by referring to your political or religious opinions or affiliations that do not directly relate to your ability to do the job. An employer might not agree with your politics or might feel that the workplace is nowhere to display attitudes that might alienate others.

- Including your Salary Demands

This should not be put on the resume - it's only used to screen a candidate out of the running or influence the employer to offer less money. Salary should not be discussed until you have had the opportunity to explain your value - in person or over the phone

- Using Incompatible File Types and Formats

Electronic resumes should be created in the most readable file for most [Internet-recruiting] systems, which is plain text or Microsoft Word.

Today's resume needs to be readable by machines, which means text needs to have a font size between 10 - 12 and a simple font style, such as Arial, Verdana, Helvetica or Microsoft SansSerif.

- Lastly, don't Sound desperate like you are begging for the job.

Conclusion

No matter what field you are looking to work in, cover letters are and should be a standard practice. Once you learn the process, it becomes a simple step you can take to ensure your resume will be viewed by the human resources department. Without one, you're setting yourself up for failure. So take a step in the right direction-take some time to learn how to write a compelling CV letter, and make sure that it grabs your future boss's attention

Job seekers sometimes wonder whether or not they need to use a cover letter at all. A cover letter should accompany each resume that you submit. Submitting a cover letter differentiates you from the other candidate who has not done so. It puts you in the unique position ahead of your competitor. Remember, the resume by itself does not convey your level of enthusiasm for the job. Your cover letter can create just the tone you need to make that homerun with the hiring manager.

about The Author

MY NAME IS . i am

Do not go yet; One last thing to do

If you enjoyed this book or found it useful I'd be very grateful if you'd post a short review on Amazon. Your support really does make a difference and I read all the reviews personally so I can get your feedback and make this book even better.

Thanks again for your support!

77338080R00029

Made in the USA
Columbia, SC
26 September 2017